BIGGEST NAMES IN SPORTS
COLIN KAEPERNICK
FOOTBALL STAR

by Hubert Walker

FOCUS
READERS.
NAVIGATOR

WWW.FOCUSREADERS.COM

Focus Readers is distributed by North Star Editions:
sales@northstareditions.com | 888-417-0195

Produced for Focus Readers by Red Line Editorial.

Photographs ©: Ted S. Warren/AP Images, cover, 1; Harry How/Getty Images Sport/Getty Images, 4–5; Marcio Jose Sanchez/AP Images, 7, 20–21; Patrick Cummings/AP Images, 8–9; Matt Cilley/AP Images, 11; Kita Wright/AP Images, 13; Jeff Chiu/AP Images, 14–15; G. Newman Lowrance/AP Images, 17; Tom Gannam/AP Images, 19; Ryan Kang/AP Images, 22; Cheriss May/Sipa/AP Images, 25; Jack Kurtz/Zuma Press/Newscom, 27; Red Line Editorial, 29

Library of Congress Cataloging-in-Publication Data
Names: Walker, Hubert, 1980- author.
Title: Colin Kaepernick : football star / by Hubert Walker.
Description: Lake Elmo, MN : Focus Readers, [2021] | Series: Biggest names
   in sports | Includes index. | Audience: Grades 4-6
Identifiers: LCCN 2020039045 (print) | LCCN 2020039046 (ebook) | ISBN
   9781644937013 (hardcover) | ISBN 9781644937372 (paperback) | ISBN
   9781644938096 (pdf) | ISBN 9781644937730 (ebook)
Subjects: LCSH: Kaepernick, Colin, 1987---Juvenile literature. |
   Quarterbacks (Football)--United States--Biography--Juvenile literature.|
   Football players--United States--Biography--Juvenile literature. | San
   Francisco 49ers (Football team)--History--Juvenile literature. |
   Political activists--United States--History--Juvenile literature. |
   Sports--Political aspects--Juvenile literature.
Classification: LCC GV939.K25 W33 2021 (print) | LCC GV939.K25 (ebook) |
   DDC 796.332092 [B]--dc23
LC record available at https://lccn.loc.gov/2020039045
LC ebook record available at https://lccn.loc.gov/2020039046

Printed in the United States of America
Mankato, MN
012021

ABOUT THE AUTHOR

Hubert Walker enjoys running, hunting, and going to the dog park with his best pal. He grew up in Georgia but moved to Minnesota in 2018. Overall, he loves his new home, but he's not a fan of the cold winters.

TABLE OF CONTENTS

SHREDDING THE CHEESEHEADS

Colin Kaepernick took the snap and scanned the field. The San Francisco 49ers quarterback couldn't find an open receiver. So, he took off. Kaepernick scrambled 20 yards and bolted into the corner of the end zone. The San Francisco crowd went wild. Kaepernick had just tied the game.

Colin Kaepernick sprints for a touchdown during a January 2013 playoff game against the Green Bay Packers.

The 49ers and the Green Bay Packers were locked in a fierce **playoff** battle in January 2013. And Kaepernick was just getting warmed up. In the second quarter, he fired a 20-yard laser to Michael Crabtree. The 49ers receiver dived into the end zone for a touchdown.

In the third quarter, Kaepernick faked a handoff. But he kept the ball and dashed to the right. Kaepernick threaded his way through Packers defenders. He sprinted into the end zone for a 56-yard touchdown run.

Kaepernick shredded the Green Bay defense all night long. He racked up 263 passing yards and 181 rushing yards.

Kaepernick prepares to pass during a playoff game against the Packers in January 2013.

The 49ers crushed the Packers 45–31. Kaepernick had shown that he was one of the most exciting players in the National Football League (NFL).

LEADER OF THE WOLF PACK

Colin Kaepernick was born on November 3, 1987, in Milwaukee, Wisconsin. His mother was white, and his father was Black. Colin's mother put him up for adoption when he was still a baby. Both of his adoptive parents were white.

When Colin was four years old, he and his family moved to Turlock, California.

Kaepernick takes the field with his parents during his senior year of college.

Growing up, Colin often experienced **racism**. Kids at school made fun of him because he didn't look like his parents. But his parents told him he should be proud of his skin color.

Meanwhile, Colin excelled at every sport he tried. He was a fierce competitor with a powerful arm. In high school, he earned all-state honors in football, basketball, and baseball.

Several colleges offered him baseball **scholarships**. But Colin didn't want to play baseball in college. He wanted to play football. Unfortunately, most **scouts** thought Colin was too skinny. Only one school offered him a football scholarship.

Kaepernick dives into the end zone during his freshman year at the University of Nevada, Reno.

He accepted the offer and attended the University of Nevada, Reno.

Kaepernick didn't have to wait long for his chance to play. When he was a freshman, Nevada's starting quarterback got hurt. Kaepernick stepped in and threw four touchdown passes in his first game.

After that, he became the Wolf Pack's full-time starter.

Kaepernick could do more than just throw. He also racked up rushing yards. By his senior year, he was one of the best running quarterbacks in college football.

OVERTIME THRILLER

Boise State is one of Nevada's biggest rivals. Unfortunately for Nevada fans, Boise State always seemed to come out on top. Most people expected that trend to continue in 2010. After all, Boise State was the No. 3 team in college football. The teams played in November that year. The Wolf Pack fell behind by 17 at halftime. But Kaepernick led his team to a thrilling overtime victory. Nevada's coach said it was the biggest win in school history.

Kaepernick stiff-arms a cornerback during a 2010 game against Louisiana Tech.

Kaepernick became the first player to pass for more than 10,000 yards and run for more than 4,000 yards.

That got the attention of NFL scouts. In the 2011 NFL **Draft**, the San Francisco 49ers selected Kaepernick in the second round. He was ready to become a pro.

DOUBLE THREAT

Colin Kaepernick didn't play much during his **rookie** season. But that changed in his second year. Starter Alex Smith suffered a head injury in Week 10 of the 2012 season. Kaepernick was ready for his chance to shine. He proved to be a double threat, just like he had been in college.

Kaepernick makes an off-balance pass under pressure during a game between the San Francisco 49ers and the St. Louis Rams.

In some games, Kaepernick beat teams with his legs. For example, he ran for a 50-yard touchdown against the Miami Dolphins in Week 14. In other games, he beat teams with his arm. Kaepernick threw four touchdown passes against the New England Patriots in Week 15.

HOT START

In his first career start, Kaepernick faced the Chicago Bears. He didn't waste any time showing what he could do. In the first quarter, he launched a 57-yard bomb to Kyle Williams. On the next play, he tossed a touchdown pass to Vernon Davis. Kaepernick finished the game with 243 passing yards and two touchdowns. San Francisco crushed the Bears 32–7.

Kaepernick finds a running lane during Super Bowl XLVII.

Smith eventually became healthy. But San Francisco stuck with Kaepernick. The second-year star led his team to the Super Bowl. In the big game, Kaepernick passed for 302 yards and one touchdown.

He ran for another 62 yards and one rushing touchdown. However, it wasn't enough. The Baltimore Ravens beat San Francisco 34–31.

Despite the tough loss, Kaepernick started off hot in 2013. In the first game of the season, he scorched Green Bay for 412 passing yards. Kaepernick led the 49ers back to the playoffs that year. They beat the Packers and the Carolina Panthers in the first two rounds. But with a trip to the Super Bowl on the line, San Francisco fell to the Seattle Seahawks.

In 2014, Kaepernick notched career highs for passing yards and rushing yards. However, the 49ers offense

Kaepernick delivers a pass to a 49ers receiver during a 2015 game against the Rams.

struggled to score points. San Francisco finished with a disappointing 8–8 record.

The team continued to go downhill in 2015. Kaepernick threw only six touchdown passes in the first eight weeks of the season. Coaches benched him in Week 9. It was a rough end to a rough season.

FROM ATHLETE TO ACTIVIST

Colin Kaepernick hoped to bounce back in 2016. But he ended up making headlines for a different reason. Before each game, Kaepernick chose to kneel during the national anthem. He was protesting against **police brutality** and racism. Football fans were sharply divided over his actions. Many said

Eric Reid (left) and Kaepernick kneel together in protest during the national anthem before a September 2016 game.

Players across the NFL followed Kaepernick's lead. In this image, several Houston Texans kneel before a 2017 game.

Kaepernick was disrespecting the US flag. Others said he was bringing attention to important issues.

Kaepernick put up solid numbers in 2016. However, San Francisco won only two games all year. When the season was over, Kaepernick ended his contract with the 49ers. That meant he was free to sign with any team that wanted him.

But when the 2017 season began, Kaepernick still didn't have a job. No teams even brought him in for a tryout. Kaepernick's stats from 2016 showed that he was better than many starting quarterbacks in the league. Yet he couldn't even get hired as a backup. Kaepernick suspected it wasn't because of his playing abilities. Instead, it was because of his protests. And if that were true, the NFL was breaking the law.

Kaepernick filed a complaint with the league. He said the NFL's owners had made a secret agreement to stop him from playing. The complaint went through a long court battle.

Meanwhile, Kaepernick kept busy. He continued to practice, hoping a team would sign him. He also turned his attention to **activism**. For example, he gave large amounts of money to several charities. One of the charities fought against police brutality. Another helped at-risk kids. Yet another served Black military veterans.

Kaepernick also started a camp called Know Your Rights. Kids who took part in the camp learned about a wide variety of topics. One class gave advice on how to calmly deal with police officers. Another class taught kids about Black history. And another class discussed healthy

Charlene Carruthers (right) helped lead BYP100, a Black activist group supported by Kaepernick.

eating. Kaepernick's goal was to help kids understand that they have the power to take control of their lives.

In 2019, Kaepernick's court battle finally ended. The NFL agreed to give him several million dollars. Even so, it was far less than Kaepernick would have earned if he had been playing.

Going into the 2020 football season, Kaepernick still hadn't been signed by an NFL team. However, he didn't regret his

SHIFTING ATTITUDES

In 2020, an unarmed Black man named George Floyd died after police pinned him to the ground. Floyd's death sparked protests across the United States. As a result, the attitudes of many white Americans shifted. Many white people started to see what Kaepernick had been talking about for years.

Wearing a Kaepernick jersey, a man kneels at the memorial site for George Floyd in Minneapolis, Minnesota.

decision to protest. It may have cost him his career. But Kaepernick believed some things were more important than football.

COLIN KAEPERNICK

- Height: 6 feet 4 inches (193 cm)
- Weight: 230 pounds (104 kg)
- Birth date: November 3, 1987
- Birthplace: Milwaukee, Wisconsin
- High school: John H. Pitman High School (Turlock, California)
- College: University of Nevada, Reno (Reno, Nevada) (2006–2010)
- NFL team: San Francisco 49ers (2011–2016)
- Major achievements: Western Athletic Conference Offensive Player of the Year (2008, 2010); most rushing yards by a quarterback in an NFL game (January 2013)

FOCUS ON
COLIN KAEPERNICK

Write your answers on a separate piece of paper.

1. Write a paragraph that summarizes the main ideas of Chapter 4.

2. Do you agree with Kaepernick's decision to kneel during the national anthem? Why or why not?

3. After the 2012 season, which team did the 49ers play in the Super Bowl?

   A. Baltimore Ravens
   B. Green Bay Packers
   C. New England Patriots

4. What made Kaepernick different from most college quarterbacks?

   A. He got a football scholarship.
   B. He was great at running the ball.
   C. He had a strong throwing arm.

Answer key on page 32.

GLOSSARY

activism

Actions to make social or political changes.

draft

A system that allows teams to acquire new players coming into a league.

playoff

One game in a series of games played after the regular season to decide which team will be the champion.

police brutality

When a police officer uses more force than necessary against civilians.

racism

Hatred or mistreatment of people because of their skin color or ethnicity.

rookie

A professional athlete in his or her first year.

scholarships

Money given to students to pay for education expenses.

scouts

People who look for talented young players.

TO LEARN MORE

BOOKS

Braun, Eric. *Colin Kaepernick: From Free Agent to Change Agent*. Minneapolis: Lerner Publications, 2020.

Harris, Duchess. *Black Lives Matter*. Minneapolis: Abdo Publishing, 2018.

Hunter, Tony. *San Francisco 49ers*. Minneapolis: Abdo Publishing, 2020.

NOTE TO EDUCATORS

Visit **www.focusreaders.com** to find lesson plans, activities, links, and other resources related to this title.

INDEX